EASY RAMBLES

AROUND
CONISTON & HAWKSHEAD

VIVIENNE CROW

QUESTA

ISBN 978-1-898808-34-3

Maps:
The maps accompanying the walks in this book are purely diagrammatic, and are based on maps produced by Harvey Maps (Licence No. 86413/1 © Harvey Map Services Ltd.)

Published by
Questa Publishing Limited
PO Box 520, BAMBER BRIDGE,
Lancashire PR5 8LF

and printed by
Carnmor Print, 95/97 London Road, Preston,
Lancashire PR1 4BA

CONTENTS

NOTE

No attempt has been made to grade the walks in this book, as this is too subjective. Use the information about distance and height gain to calculate how long the walk will take.

INTRODUCTION

The area to the west of Windermere around Hawkshead and Coniston is a dream come true for ramblers - soft, rolling countryside, with attractive woodland and twinkling tarns, that suddenly yields to more dramatic, craggy scenery as you head further north. Deer quietly graze the lower slopes and squirrels rummage in the undergrowth while, all around, the sound of birdsong fills the woods. And every step you take is a step back in time – from Donald Campbell's ill-fated speed attempts in the 1960s back through Beatrix Potter, John Ruskin and the grand schemes of the Victorians to the early miners, the powerful monks of Furness Abbey and even Bronze Age settlers.

The Lake District is essentially a massive volcanic dome fissured by tectonic forces and then sculpted by huge rivers of ice to create a spray of valleys and dividing mountain ranges radiating from a central hub – a bit like spokes from a wheel. One of these glaciers would have gouged out the deep, u-shaped valley that holds Windermere – and the same goes for Coniston Water too. When the ice finally melted, more than 10,000 years ago, the water filled the remaining hollow, forming the lakes that exists today.

The retreating ice sheets left a barren landscape that was slowly colonised by hardy plants such as juniper, mosses and grasses. The area's natural vegetation cover would have become established only about 7,000-8,000 years ago: oak and elm forest on the lower fells and then pine and birch woodland up to an altitude of about 2,000ft. If it hadn't been for man's intervention, that is exactly what you would see around Hawkshead and Coniston today – a mass of trees with just the rocky tops poking through the woods.

Although there is little solid evidence of Stone Age man in the immediate area, it is thought that this is when humans first began to settle here. As well as growing crops, Neolithic man was the first to start creating clearings in the forest for his livestock. These animals grazed on the native flora, restricting its growth and slowing the rate of natural regeneration, a process that has continued ever since. The arrival of the 'Beaker' people early in the second millennium BC heralded the start of the Bronze Age, and more extensive clearances. The climate was considerably warmer and calmer in the early to mid-Bronze Age, allowing man to avoid the dense, lower forests where bears and wolves would have roamed, and to live higher up the fells. Many Bronze Age sites in the Lake District are located at about 500 to 1,200ft above sea level – including Banishead, Bleathwaite and Torver High Common, all to the west of Coniston Water.

Celts, Romans, Anglo-Saxons and Norsemen all made their mark on the area too - and, with the exception of the Romans, left their calling cards in the form of place names. Many of the names of the topographical features, for example, are Celtic in origin – 'glen' meaning valley, for example, appears throughout the district; and 'creic' becomes crag. The influence of Germanic settlers is evident in place names ending in 'ton' - from the Anglian word 'tun' meaning farmstead. And then there were the Vikings – look at a map of Norway today and you will quickly discover why the Cumbrians call their hills and mountains fells; 'fjell' means mountain in Norwegian. The Norse word for waterfall is 'foss', which becomes 'force' in the Lake District; 'tjorn' becomes tarn; and 'bekkr' beck.

In medieval times, the area between Windermere and the eastern shore of Coniston Water was controlled by the wealthy monks of Furness Abbey, while the lands to the west were initially signed over to the Baron of Kendal when the partitioning of Coniston was ratified by Richard I in 1196. The hard-working Cistercian monks had a profound impact on the area, bringing trade and industry on a scale never seen before. It was the abbey that was behind the establishment of Hawkshead's market, which became an important centre for the wool trade. It also set up primitive iron smelters, known as 'bloomeries', which were dependant on the area's hazel and oak woodland for charcoal. Although the Dissolution of the Monasteries in the 16th century was a social disaster for Cumbria - schools were closed and poor relief abandoned - the economy didn't collapse. In fact, this was about the time that the woollen industry really began to peak, and it is also when mining took off, encouraged by a national policy of fostering defence and industry.

You can't fail to be aware of the impact of the mining and quarrying industries on this part of the Lake District as you walk the routes in this book, particularly those to the west of the area, around Coniston. The Old Man has, in fact, been likened to a holey cheese because of the lumps and chunks that have been torn out of it in the search for both copper and slate over the years. The Coniston village walk and the route on to Holme Fell, in particular, give walkers a taste of some of this industrial archaeology, including the huge caverns of the Hodge Close workings.

The routes in this book, roughly in ascending order of difficulty, give a taste of the rich and varied landscape around Hawkshead and Coniston, while also introducing walkers to the area's fascinating natural and human history. Some walks follow gentle lakeshore paths with the water lapping at your feet, others head into the wonderful forests and woods that characterise this area. The Holme Fell, Carron Crag, Latterbarrow and Blawith Knott walks all climb easily accessible, low summits for some fantastic views of the fells, both near and far. If you want to escape the crowds, try lonely Torver Common or Blawith Knott. Some of the prettiest tarns in the whole of the Lake District can be seen on the Tarn Hows and Claife Heights walks. The latter also includes a long section of track beside wonderful Windermere, as does the Wray Castle route. And no visit to the area would be complete without dropping in on the two main villages: walk numbers four and five take in lovely Hawkshead, where there are plenty of pubs and cafés to tempt you to linger; while the first route in the book leads the walker on an historical tour of Coniston. Enjoy!

1

CONISTON VILLAGE

This gentle saunter around the edge of Coniston and up to the attractive waterfalls on Church Beck provides a good overview of the west of the area as well as a feel for the history of the place. Walkers head right up to the very base of the craggy Yewdale Fells and look up into the Coppermines Valley before returning via a low fellside path - with good views over the lake - and a disused railway. The walk can be rounded off with a visit to John Ruskin's grave in St Andrew's churchyard.

Start/Finish: Main pay and display car park near the Tourist Information Centre in Coniston (SD303975)
Distance: 4.7km (2.9 miles)
Height gain: 156m (510ft)

---

1. Leave the car park, turn left along the minor road and, almost immediately, turn right along the B5285. Just before the road narrows to cross Yewdale Beck, turn left along Shepherds Bridge Lane. At the main road – the A593 – cross diagonally over to pick up a narrow lane heading towards the Holly How youth hostel. Follow the lane round to the right, and, as soon as you reach a row of cottages, turn left up a rough track climbing beside the buildings.

2. At the top, go through the small gate and turn left. You are now on a lovely path that hugs the base of the Yewdale Fells. Once through the next gate, turn right along the rough lane, towards the Coppermines Valley.

> *The land over the wall to your left here belongs to Holywath House. Originally just a small cottage, it was enlarged in the 1840s by John Barratt, a mining engineer*

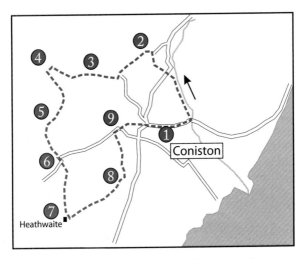

who helped develop the Coniston Mine into a thriving business.

Over the years, these grounds have been home to several mills powered by the waters of Church Beck. In the 18th century, there was a carding mill here, employing up to 30 people washing and combing wool before it went off for weaving. Known as Boon Beck or High Mill, it became a bobbin mill in the 1840s, making bobbins for the textile industries of Lancashire and Yorkshire. There was another bobbin mill further downstream, as well as a corn mill.

3. Having crossed a cattle grid, you climb gradually until the wall on your left disappears and you are able to look straight down into the deep gorge carved by Church Beck. A little further upstream are some impressive falls. Be very careful here, because the unguarded drop is extremely steep. If you continued following this track upstream, it would eventually lead into the Coppermines Valley.

This area, as its name suggests, was once the scene of a busy copper mining industry. The Romans are thought to have been the first to work the mineral veins here, and mining was definitely going on in Norman times, but it was only in the 16th century, when the German miners were invited to the area by Elizabeth I, that things really began to take off. The most prosperous period was the middle of the 19th century, when the men were working at depths of up to 1,100ft beneath the surface – that's about 500ft below sea level! At one time, there were as many as 600 people working here, including children who were involved in sorting and dressing the ore as it came out of the mine.

Growing imports of cheap ore from abroad in the 1880s marked the beginning of the end for the mine. The pumps that kept the shafts free of water were finally switched off in 1892 and, within five years, most of the mine had filled with water. Attempts were still being made to breathe new life into the industry well into the 20th century, most notably when a French count set up an operation to re-process the waste copper left on the spoil heaps, but all were short-lived.

4. At the top of the falls, leave the track by crossing the gated bridge on your left, known as Miners Bridge. There are two paths heading off to the left on the other side of the beck. Ignore the clear track heading downhill; the path you want is to the right of the short section of drystone wall.

5. The narrow fellside path, which provides views over Coniston village and the northern end of Coniston Water, eventually drops to a footbridge over Scrow Beck. Go through the large wooden gate over to your left and then climb alongside the wall. Once through the kissing-gate, keep close to the wall on your left.

6. Turn right along the minor road for about 50 metres and then, when it bends sharp right, keep straight ahead along a rough track, towards Heathwaite. Don't be tempted by the narrow trail off to the left through the trees in a short while; instead, cross the stile next to the gate straight ahead and follow a faint grassy track heading generally SSW.

7. As you approach the buildings at Heathwaite, turn left and walk down the steep, grassy slope, keeping close to the tiny beck on your right. Turn left along the surfaced track. Looking down to your right, you should be able to make out Coniston Hall near the edge of the lake, easily identified from its unusual chimney pots.

> Parts of Coniston Hall date back to the early 15th century, although a house may have existed on the site since about 1250. For centuries, it was the seat of the le Flemings, the Lords of the Manor of Coniston. It remained the property of the Fleming Estate until it was sold to the National Trust in 1971.

8. Turn right at a T-junction to cross a bridge over the disused railway. Go through a gap in the wall on your left to pick up the route of the old railway, along which you turn right. You soon walk through a housing area and pass what is left of the old Coniston station on your left.

> This branch line of the Furness Railway was opened in 1859 to link Coniston with the main line at Broughton. It must have come as a great relief to the managers of the Coniston Mining Company, who had previously had to arrange for ore and slate from the copper mines and quarries to be moved by barge down the lake or by horse and cart to the Ulverston canal. When all operations finally ceased in the late 1940s, the railway continued to operate for a few more years, bringing tourists into the area. It was finally closed in the early 1960s.

9. Turn right at the T-junction and then take the next road turning on your left, passing the Sun Inn. Turn left along the main road to cross Church Beck and then turn right, towards Brantwood and Hawkshead. You pass St Andrew's Church, the final resting place of John Ruskin, and then follow the road round to the right. Take the next turning on your right to return to the car park.

> *John Ruskin's grave can be found on the eastern edge of St Andrew's churchyard. The great Victorian intellectual had declined the prospect of a burial in Westminster Abbey and chose to remain in his beloved Lake District. His grave is marked by a large carved cross made from green Tilberthwaite slate and decorated with symbols depicting important aspects of Ruskin's life. It was designed by his secretary W G Collingwood, who was an expert on Anglo-Saxon and Norse crosses. Collingwood and his family are buried nearby. See walk nine for more information on John Ruskin's life and his home at nearby Brantwood.*

ST ANDREW'S CHURCH

St Andrew's Church was constructed in 1819 – on the site of a simple stone chapel built in 1586 by the le Fleming family. Additions were made in the late 19th century when the Rev C Chapman set his sights on a grand Gothic church. Despite his fundraising efforts, he had to settle for less – a new chancel and vestry at the eastern end of the building, a large porch and the complete refurbishment of the interior.

Before the influx of miners to Coniston, the Anglican church was the village's only place of worship. Between 1837 and 1875 though, as the population shot up, a Baptist chapel, Methodist chapel and, with the coming of the Irish miners, a Catholic church were built.

2

TORVER COMMONS AND CONISTON WATER

Peaceful farm lanes, verdant commons, magical woodland and a lovely stretch of lakeside walking are all encompassed on this gorgeous stroll from Torver, just south of Coniston. The route is generally well-signposted, there is very little climbing and boggy patches are almost non-existent – your greatest difficulty lies in deciding which of the tiny village's two pubs to visit at the end of the walk.

> Start/Finish: Torver village hall car park (SD284943)
> Distance: 7.7km (4.8 miles)
> Height gain: 156m (511ft)

1. Turn left out of the car park, soon passing the church and the Church House Inn on your left. Turn left at the first road junction – towards Greenodd and Ulverston – and, after just 100m, turn right along a surfaced bridleway, the beginning of which is set back slightly from the road. Take the next turning on your left and, when this lane bends right, leave it by going through the right-hand of the two gates on your left.

2. You are now on a narrow path between hedges on your right and a fence on your left. Keeping to this clear path, you go through a series of gates until you come to a bridge. It is possible to cut a corner here by crossing Torver Beck, following the lane and then turning right along the main road for 350m, but it is much more pleasant to miss out the road and continue to Torver Low Common. So, ignoring the bridge, carry on along the track, which soon climbs at an easy angle to a gate.

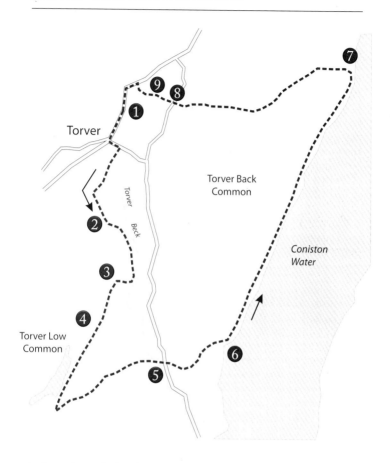

3. Once through the gate you are on the commons – a green carpet of low, rolling hummocks. It is not obvious at first which way to go. The wall on your right, which you follow for a few paces, soon bends round to the right. Just before it does so, head up the short slope to the left. There is an indistinct fork at the top where you should bear left. Don't worry if you don't spot the fork; basically, you want to head

up the gentle, grassy slope towards the wall to your left – about 10m short of the wall, the path becomes a lot clearer.

4. When the wall on your left does a sharp turn to the left, continue straight on in a SSW direction. The clear path soon passes to the left of a disused reservoir. As you approach the SE corner of the small reservoir – and just before the path fords its outlet stream – turn left along a narrow path through the bracken. This quickly joins up with the Cumbria Way coming in from the right. Continue downstream – through an attractive valley dotted with juniper bushes. The path leads to a footbridge across Torver Beck. Turn sharp right and follow the wall up to a kissing-gate, beyond which you reach the road.

5. Cross straight over and turn right along the wide farm track. This ends at a gate at the top of the rise, but the path beyond is clear as it drops down to Coniston Water. You reach the lake close to a wooden jetty.

> Look to the south and you should be able to see Peel Island. Aficionados of Arthur Ransome's famous children's story Swallows and Amazons, published in 1930, will tell you that this might be the island on which Ransome based his fictional Wildcat Island. (They will also tell you that Wildcat Island might, in fact, be Blake Holme on Windermere. Ransome's settings combined elements of both lakes.) The first in a series of books about childhood adventures, Swallows and Amazons tells the story of the Walker children, who have a dinghy called Swallow, and the Blackett youngsters, who sail Amazon. It is the school holidays and the Walkers are staying on a farm near a lake, while the Blacketts live on the opposite shore. The children meet on an island in the middle of the lake, and have a series of memorable adventures.
>
> Peel Island also features in W G Collingwood's Thorstein of the Mere: A Saga of the Northmen in Lakeland, first

published in 1895. This was one of Ransome's favourite childhood books, and the two men later became friends. Collingwood, who moved to the Lake District after a brilliant academic career at Oxford, was a pupil of Ruskin, and became his secretary in 1881.

Coniston Water will be forever linked with the memory of Donald Campbell who died on the lake in 1967 while attempting a world water-speed record, but he wasn't the first Campbell to break records on Coniston Water; his father, Sir Malcolm Campbell, achieved a record-breaking speed of 141.74mph on August 19, 1939 in Blue Bird K4. Campbell junior then hit the dizzy heights of 202.32mph on July 23, 1955 in Bluebird K7 on Ullswater in the north Lakes. He went on to achieve a further four world records on Coniston Water between 1956 and 1959. His two greatest achievements were a 1964 land speed record of 403.10mph achieved in Australia and, also in Australia in the same year, a water-speed record of 276.33mph. He finally came to grief on Coniston Water on January 4, 1967. While attempting to break the 300mph barrier, Bluebird K7 slowly lifted out of the water, did a backward somersault in the air and then plummeted into the lake nose first, killing Campbell instantly. Said to be travelling at 328mph at the time of the accident, Campbell shouted over his radio link: 'I'm going, I'm on my back... I'm gone.' His last words. A later trawl of the lake failed to find his body, but, in 2001, a team of divers brought the wreck of Bluebird to the surface. The same team went back a few months later and recovered Campbell's remains. He has since been buried in the village cemetery.

6. Follow the shore path for about 2km, in and out of atmospheric woodland. Having gone through two small gates along the way and just before another wooden jetty, you reach a finger post indicating a clear junction of paths. Turn left here – towards Torver.

7. Follow the clear track gently uphill through the woods, ignoring a branch off to the right which fords the beck. You will go through several gates. Just after the one near the idyllic farmhouse of Brackenbarrow, turn left along the rough, shady track. Cross straight over at the road and then over the stile beside the wooden gate.

8. The path isn't obvious here, but it veers right; down towards some old wooden posts close to a tumbledown wall. Go through the kissing-gate just beyond the posts and then drop into the trench that used to be home to the old Furness Railway.

> *This was part of the Coniston branch line of the Furness Railway, which had a station and goods yard at Torver.*

9. There are wooden walkways to guide walkers across the soggy ground here. As you leave the last section of board, veer right to cross a pretty meadow with a fence on your right. Turn left at the road and the car park is just 300 metres ahead on your left.

> *Torver was originally a Norse settlement and is said to get its name from the Norse word for turf.*

THE FIRST VIKINGS

It is generally believed that the first Vikings came into the area some time before the second half of the ninth century. These weren't the raping, pillaging Danish raiders of modern mythology, but Norse settlers who had come from Norway via Ireland and the Isle of Man. While the Anglo-Saxon settlers farmed the valleys around the mountain fringes, these pastoralist Norsemen began making their homes in the uplands.

3

WRAY CASTLE
AND WINDERMERE LAKESHORE

After a lovely stroll beside England's longest natural lake, this route visits the Gothic-style Wray Castle, crosses some gently undulating countryside between Low and High Wray and then enters the dark Claife forests.

Start/Finish: Lakeshore parking area at Red Nab,
near High Wray (SD385994)
Distance: 8.1km (5 miles)
Height gain: 207m (679ft)

---

1. Standing facing the water, head up the surfaced lakeshore track to your left. As you continue walking beside beautiful Windermere, the fells above Ambleside are clearly visible at the top end of the lake.

> *At nearly 17km long, Windermere is England's longest natural lake. It was created by the ice sheets of the last glacial period, which ended about 10,000 years ago. A glacier, which formed in the central part of the Lake District gouged out a deep, u-shaped valley as it ploughed southwards. This later filled with water to create the lake we see today.*

> *The lake is home, all year round, to mute swan, moorhen, coot, mallard and merganser. Grebe – little and great crested – tufted duck and cormorant can also be seen. Wintering species include teal, goldeneye, goosander and both Canada and greylag geese.*

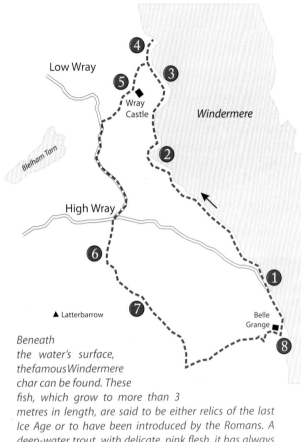

Low Wray

Wray
Castle

Windermere

Blelham Tarn

High Wray

▲ Latterbarrow

Belle
Grange

Beneath
the water's surface,
the famous Windermere
char can be found. These
fish, which grow to more than 3
metres in length, are said to be either relics of the last
Ice Age or to have been introduced by the Romans. A
deep-water trout, with delicate, pink flesh, it has always
been regarded as something of a delicacy. Princes and
politicians at the royal court would have tucked into it
during medieval times, and char pies were once regarded
as a very fashionable gift among the aristocracy. Today,
potted char can occasionally be found on menus at local

restaurants. The season runs from March to September when the fish are caught using two rods and shiny metal spinners.

2. Soon after going through a gate close to the second boathouse that you pass, the track begins climbing away from the lake. As it does so, go through the gate on your right – to gain access to the permitted footpath to Wray Castle. There is no path on the ground now, but continue walking with the water on your right. Just before you reach a tree-covered crag that comes right down to the water's edge, you will need to climb the gravelly slope up to your left. At the top, swing right to enter the woods via a gate. The path soon drops back down towards the water's edge and swings left.

3. Pass a wooden boathouse to reach a clear track. The main route heads left, but first take a short detour to the right to visit the interesting old Wray Castle Boathouse and then go through a kissing-gate into Calf Parrock Coppice and out to an interesting crag in the woods.

4. From the coppice, return to the signpost at the boathouse junction and then keep right to walk with the railings on your right. Bear right at the next fork, and the path comes out on a driveway in front of Wray Castle.

This huge, Gothic-style house and the neighbouring church were built in the 1840s by a Dr Dawson, a retired Liverpool surgeon, using his wife's inheritance. It is said that she took one look at it when it was finished and refused to live there. The building is not open to the public.

The imposing house is intricately linked with the birth of the National Trust. When Dawson died in 1875, his nephew, Preston Rawnsley, inherited the estate. Preston's cousin was Hardwicke Rawnsley, who became one of the co-founders of the National Trust. He took up the appointment of vicar of Wray Church in 1877. Five years later, in 1882, a 16-year-old Beatrix Potter and her family spent their summer holiday at the castle, and it was while they were here that she was introduced to Hardwicke Rawnsley. Their subsequent friendship had a profound effect on Potter's attitude towards the countryside and the need to preserve it for future generations - so much so, in fact, that when she died in 1943 she left 14 farms and 4,000 acres of land to the National Trust.

5. Turn right and, when you reach the gatehouse, turn left along the minor road. Soon after passing the road turning to the Windermere Ferry in the peaceful hamlet of High Wray, turn left along a rough track – towards the National Trust's 'Basecamp'. Climbing gently, the track reaches the forest edge at a fork. Bear left here and, as the track enters the grounds of the camp, turn right through a gate.

> *Every year, the National Trust relies on an army of volunteers to carry out path repairs and work on its properties in the area. Many of these are housed at 'Basecamp'.*

6. Follow the line of a wall on your left and then enter the forest proper via a deer gate. Ignore a turning on your right a few metres into the forest and follow the narrow path as it winds its way deeper into the trees on a soft bed of golden pine needles.

7. After the next deer gate, turn right along a sometimes muddy path. Bear left along a wide forest track and then turn left again at the next path junction – towards Belle Grange.

8. At the end of this track, close to the edge of the lake again, turn left. As you pass between two gate posts in about 0.75km, the car park is on your right.

4

GRIZEDALE FOREST AND HAWKSHEAD

A stroll across a tiny corner of the immense Grizedale Forest is followed by a walk along farm paths through lovely, rolling countryside in the South Lakes. The route drops down into Hawkshead where you can get refreshments from any one of a large number of pubs and cafés before heading out to Howe Farm near Esthwaite Water and then climbing back up to Hawkshead Moor. Apart from a brief section after leaving the forest, all the paths are well signposted and easy to follow. There are a few short, easy climbs along the way, the hardest of which comes near the end of the walk.

Start/Finish: Moor Top car park in Grizedale Forest (SD342965)
Distance: 7.1km (4.4 miles)
Height gain: 219m (718ft)

---

1. As you head into the forest, the wide forest road splits just beyond the wooden barrier. Bear right – towards Hawkshead. When you reach a three-way split, take the middle option – a narrower track heading gently uphill. Rejoining the forest road, turn right and then, almost immediately, right again. At almost 250m above sea level, this is the highest point on the walk.

> *Like much of this area, the woods around Grizedale used to belong to the wealthy monks of Furness Abbey, and, in the early 16th century, it became a deer park. The Forestry Commission has owned the land since the 1930s.*

2. After passing a small pool in the trees to your left, you join a wider track. Ignore a path to the right here. At the next junction, go straight

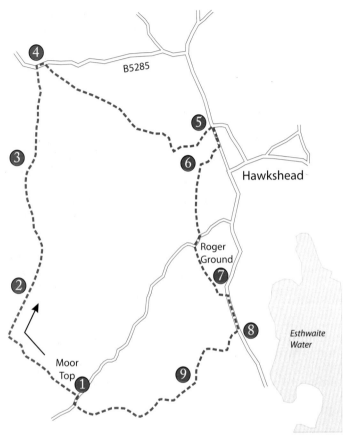

across, continuing in the same direction on a narrow path through the trees.

3. Leave the confines of the forest via a small gate in the boundary fence, and follow an indistinct path beside the beck. When you reach

what looks like a junction of paths, bear left across the beck and through a kissing-gate. There is no path on the ground now, but keep heading N and you will soon see a marker post just to the left of a pair of trees straight ahead. Continue N from here, aiming just to the left of a power line pole. When you reach a rough farm track, turn right and then left through a kissing-gate. Continue N, towards the wall on your right, where you will pick up a narrow path leading to the road.

4. Go through the wooden gate and then through the kissing-gate on your immediate right - towards Hawkshead. The path soon crosses a concrete farm track and drops to a kissing-gate. It crosses a couple of small footbridges and then swings left to follow the beck downstream for a short while. Follow the fence until it kinks left. Now go through the awkward kissing-gate straight ahead to walk with a fence on your right. Beyond the next kissing-gate, follow the fence on your left down to a surfaced lane, along which you turn left.

5. At the bottom of Vicarage Lane in Hawkshead, turn right to pass to the right of the Co-op, then head diagonally across the square to walk with the Market Hall Meeting Room on your left. Enter the churchyard and, as you pass the church on your left, swing right to walk below a burial area on a small hill.

> St Michael and All Angels Church was built in the 15th century, although there have been improvements and additions since then.
>
> Close to the church is Hawkshead's old grammar school, a free school that was established in 1585 by Edwin Sandys, of nearby Esthwaite Hall. Sandys spent some time as a prisoner in the Tower of London under Mary Tudor, but then became Archbishop of York under Elizabeth I. The school's most famous pupil was William Wordsworth.
>
> The young poet boarded with Ann Tyson while he was at the school, first in a beautiful 16th-century cottage in the

middle of the village and then out at Colthouse. Having lost his mother a few years earlier, Wordsworth adored the kind and maternal Mrs Tyson and described her in The Prelude as "my old Dame, so motherly and good..."

6. Leave the church grounds and head towards another gate, beyond which you turn left – towards Roger Ground. A well-defined trail leads through a series of kissing-gates to a minor road, along which you turn right. Walk uphill for 100m. When the road bends sharp right, turn left along a narrow lane – towards Howe Farm. Keep to the lane, even when it seems like you're heading down someone's private drive. When you reach a gate with a "Private" sign on it, cross the small bridge to the right and follow the fence on your left to the farm.

7. When you reach the buildings, go through the gate on the left and follow the path round to the right to reach the farm track. Turn left and then right along the road.

The lake on the left is Esthwaite Water, a relatively shallow body of water that is about 2.5km long and just a few hundred metres wide. It is home to the largest trout fishery in the north-west of England and, as such, is one of the most popular fishing spots in the area.

It is hoped that salmon will one day return to the lake. The fish cages at Hawkshead Trout Farm have been removed and the fishery is moving from stocking rainbow trout to native brown trout in a bid to return the lake to a more natural state. Improved water quality and the long-term removal of non-indigenous species will ultimately allow the removal of the fish screen on Cunsey Beck, which currently prevents the movement of rainbow trout downstream to Windermere. This in turn will enable salmon to migrate through Esthwaite Water to their natural spawning grounds in the headwaters above the lake.

8. Walk along the road for 300m and then turn right along the second of two tracks running parallel with each other. The track soon swings left to pass to the right of a white cottage and then goes through a large gate – this time it really does enter someone's front yard. Go through the gate to the left of the building and then walk up the rough track beside the beck.

9. After leaving the wooded area, follow the clearly waymarked trail, which swings left to climb the grassy hillside. Twisting and turning all the way, the path eventually leads up to some buildings. Follow the wide vehicle track all the way to the road. Turn right and the parking area is on the left.

RED SQUIRRELS

Red squirrels can occasionally still be spotted in Grizedale Forest. Cumbria is one of the last strongholds of these cute, fluffy-tailed creatures. In most of the rest of England and Wales they have been replaced by their grey cousins, introduced from North America in 1876. Partly because greys breed rapidly, with two litters a year, and are better able to survive a severe winter because of their extra body fat, they out-compete the reds, particularly in lowland deciduous woodland. They have been known to displace the native species completely within seven years of arrival in a wood. Red squirrels are also more susceptible to certain diseases, particularly the devastating squirrelpox virus, and find it less easy to adapt when hedgerows and woodland are destroyed.

Large conifer plantations provide red squirrels with a competitive advantage over greys. This is because, unlike in diverse broadleaf woodland, the only significant food source are the small seeds from conifer cones. With greys roughly twice the body weight of reds, these are insufficient for the invaders' needs.

5

LATTERBARROW

At a mere 244 metres, Latterbarrow is barely worthy of the title 'fell', but it's the views from the top that make this little bump in the landscape a grand destination on a clear day. You're unlikely to have the summit to yourself – it's a popular walk from busy Hawkshead – but don't let that spoil your enjoyment as you slowly turn 360 degrees at the top to take in your surroundings. Most of the paths are well signposted and easy to follow. The climb to the summit is steep, but short-lived.

Start/Finish: Main pay and display car park
in Hawkshead (SD353980)
Distance: 6.8km (4.2 miles)
Height gain: 231m (758ft)

---

1. With your back to the toilet block near the main 'pay and display' car parks, turn left and then right, into the village. Walk between the National Trust shop and the Queen's Head Inn. Just after the Red Lion's tiny beer garden, turn right along a lane and, as this ends, swing left to go through a small gate.

2. Cross straight over the road and down the track opposite. After crossing the beck via a narrow footbridge, turn left. Almost immediately, strike off right, across the grass, to a kissing-gate in the field corner. Continue in roughly the same direction to another kissing-gate, beyond which you bear left. You will return to this point from the other direction near the end of the walk.

3. The path leads to a rough, fenced track along which you turn left. Almost immediately, go through a kissing-gate on your right. Passing through more kissing-gates along the way, you will reach Loanthwaite

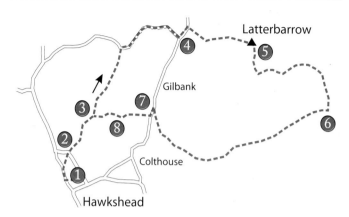

Lane, along which you turn right. Occasional gaps in the hedge on the left provide good views of the Fairfield Horseshoe and, to the east of these fells, Red Screes.

4. At the T-junction, turn left and then right through a gate with a fingerpost beside it. A clear path heads gently uphill and, when this forks, bear left to climb more steeply. The well-trodden trail swings right to reach the tall column at the summit of Latterbarrow where the far-ranging view includes the Coniston Fells, Crinkle Crags, the Langdale Pikes, the peaks of the Fairfield Horseshoe and some of the eastern fells.

The name Latterbarrow comes from the old Norse and means 'hill where animals have their lair'.

5. Swing half-right to follow the wide track down through the bracken (S). At the bottom of the slope, cross the wooden stile and follow the track through the woods. Beyond a gap in a drystone wall, you enter a felled area. Keep to the track when it soon swings right. It then curves left to reach a rise where you can again see the fells to the NE. At the next wall corner, follow the track as it swings right again for a few metres and then crosses a gap in a wall. It drops down some steps,

27

crosses an open area and then follows a wall back up to the forest proper.

6. Turn right along the gravel track - towards Hawkshead. The track forks on a couple of occasions, but the separate branches always meet up again, so it doesn't matter which option you choose.

7. Turn left at the road and then right along a narrow lane. About 70m beyond the junction, turn left at a fingerpost and go through a wooden gate. Swing right to walk with a fence on your left and then go through a gap in the wall. There isn't an obvious path on the ground now, but if you look W, you should be able to see a yellow-topped marker post. Make your way over to this and then continue W, past the next marker post and across a stone stile in a wall. Follow the path downhill to Scar House Lane.

8. Cross straight over the track to go through a kissing-gate a little to the right. At the next junction of paths, bear left and go through the kissing-gate to retrace your steps to the start of the walk.

> *Hawkshead has existed since the 10th century. It is named after the Norseman Haukr who is thought to have built its earliest dwellings. Today it is an attractive, jumbled muddle of narrow alleyways, low archways, timber-framed buildings and a market square. The market, which was initially an important centre for the wool trade, was first established by the wealthy monks of Furness Abbey. At one time, all the land in the area belonged to the monks.*

> *They were also responsible for building Hawkshead Hall just to the north of the village. All that now remains of the medieval manor house is the National Trust-owned Old Courthouse, which was once its gatehouse. The villagers would come here to pay their rents and tithes, and wrongdoers would be tried and punished.*

6

Tarn Hows and Monk Coniston

Despite being man-made, Tarn Hows is one of the most popular beauty spots in the whole of the Lake District. And it is well worth a visit, especially if you come at it from the south. This walk does exactly that, starting from the northern end of Coniston Water, passing through the lovely Monk Coniston arboretum and then gently climbing good tracks through attractive woodland until you are standing looking down on this picturesque Victorian creation. Having completed a circuit of Tarn Hows, the route then returns via a quiet road and pleasant farm paths.

> Start/Finish: Lake District National Park's Monk Coniston
> pay and display car park at the northern end of Coniston Water
> (SD316978)
> Distance: 7.6km (4.7 miles)
> Height gain: 245m (803ft)

1. From the parking area, walk to the road, cross straight over and go through the gate opposite. A grassy path heads gently uphill through National Trust land. Go through the small gate in the metal railings and follow the gravel path round to the right, up through the arboretum. At a junction close to the walled garden, go through the gate in the wall. Continue straight ahead to a T-junction of paths and then turn left to exit the gardens via a tall metal gate. Head downhill, crossing straight over a track, and then keep right – along a track through the trees, signposted Tarn Hows.

> *The arboretum here was planted by James Garth Marshall, a Leeds industrialist who had made his money from the flax-spinning industry. He bought the 700-acre Monk Coniston estate from the Knott family in 1835. The*

original building on the site of the current hall is said to have been constructed by the monks of Furness Abbey in the 13th century.

2. Cross the minor road and head straight up the trail climbing gently through the woods. Soon after crossing a narrow, dam-like footbridge, the track climbs some steps to a T-junction. Turn right along the permitted bridleway. Turn left at the next T-junction, along a permitted cycleway. Bear right at a fork in the track, and then turn left at a path junction close to the edge of the trees.

3. You soon reach a minor road looking down over Tarn Hows. Cross

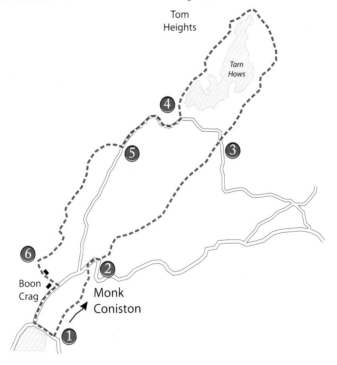

straight over – into the disabled parking area and then along the surfaced track. Take the next track on your left, which has a barrier across it. Once through the gate at the bottom, bear right along the clear track to continue your circuit of Tarn Hows. The constructed path goes all the way around it.

> *With plans based on the ideas of the 'picturesque' that were popular at the time, James Marshall created Tarn Hows by damming one of the original three tiny tarns on the site to create the single body of water that exists today. He also planted the conifer plantations that surround it, intending both to frame and reveal views of his new creation.*

4. Beyond the gate at the south-western edge of the water, take the middle of the three paths. Just after you join a path coming in from the right, bear right at a fork. Turn right along the road, crossing a cattle grid just beyond the main car park. The road winds its way down the hillside with superb views across to Wetherlam on the other side of the valley.

5. Turn right, through a kissing-gate and along a clear track, towards Low Yewdale. As the track swings sharp right to drop to a cottage, go through the large gate on your left. The faint grassy path, muddy in places, heads away from the wall in a SSW direction. Beyond the first field, it goes through a gate and then keeps fairly close to some woods on the right. When the fence on the right swings away, the path swings left. Just a few metres beyond the next gate/stile, the path – indistinct at this point – swings sharp left to pass to the left of a group of large trees.

> *As you descend, with Coniston Water directly ahead, you will soon be able to see Monk Coniston below to the left. In 1926, as the Marshall family fortunes declined, the house and gardens were sold to John Perry Bradshaw. Beatrix Potter bought the rest of the estate, including all the farmland and Tarn Hows, in 1930. Almost immediately,*

she sold half at cost price to the National Trust; and the other half passed to the charity after her death in 1943. The National Trust purchased the hall and gardens in 1945, re-uniting the estate once more.

6. Beyond the gate at the bottom of the path, turn left along the rough track, soon passing Boon Crag Farm. Turn right at the road and then, almost immediately, go through the gap on your right to pick up a permitted bridleway. This runs parallel with the road all the way to Coniston, but you follow it only until it approaches the lakeshore. When it does so, go through the gap in the hedge on your left and take the road turning on the left, towards Brantwood. The car park is about 200 metres along this road on your right.

GONDOLA

A pleasant way to see Coniston Water is from the National Trust's restored steam yacht, Gondola. The original Gondola was first launched in 1859 by Sir James Ramsden, a director of the Furness Railway Company. She carried tourists up and down the length of the lake until 1936, when she was decommissioned. She then became a houseboat until a storm ripped her from her moorings and beached her in the early 1960s. She was finally restored and relaunched in 1980. Today, Gondola carries passengers between Coniston Pier and the Brantwood and Monk Coniston jetties, a round trip of about 45 minutes. There are also occasional 90-minute cruises along the full length of Coniston Water, during which visitors learn about some of the most famous people associated with Coniston – John Ruskin, Donald Campbell, Arthur Ransome et al.

7

BLAWITH KNOTT

*To the south-west of the bottom tip of Coniston Water is a lovely area
of low fells that stretch on for miles. Tiny tarns hide in secluded hollows
surrounded by heather and bracken, and the whole area is criss-crossed
by a network of narrow trails and good bridleways. This route explores
just a tiny area of these delightful commons.*

Start/Finish: The walk starts from where the Tottlebank to
Heathwaite bridleway crosses the minor road near the
Giant's Grave (SD256878). There is roadside parking to be had in
several places nearby, and there is room for two or three cars on the
grass verge about 200 metres south of the start point
Distance: 6.3km (3.9 miles)
Height gain: 282m (926ft)

1. Where the Tottlebank to Heathwaite bridleway crosses the minor
road near the Giant's Grave, walk north along the road (downhill) for
a few metres. When the road begins to swing left, turn right along a
wide, grassy track (NNE). This eventually climbs to the top of Blawith
Knott. If you keep to the main path all the way, you will come across a
steep section that has been badly eroded by off-road motorcyclists –
a major problem on these fells. It gets very muddy and slippery in wet
weather, but the worst of it can be easily avoided by heading up on to
the rockier ground to your left.

> *This area was once covered in woodland – Blawith actually
> means 'dark wood'. Most of the trees would have been
> felled by the 17th century. They were coppiced for charcoal,
> which, in turn, was used in the iron-smelting industry. The
> iron ore used to be carried up from the Furness mines to*

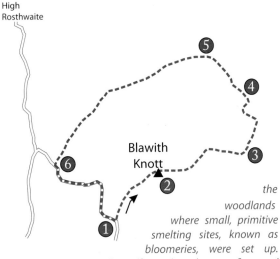

High
Rosthwaite

Blawith
Knott

*the
woodlands
where small, primitive
smelting sites, known as
bloomeries, were set up.
These extremely inefficient hearths were first used
by Iron Age man and would consume many acres
of woodland to smelt just one ton of iron. Even by
the time the Furness Abbey monks came along, the
technique had changed little. Efficiency improved
slightly with the invention of the bellows, but even
then it was a marginal change. Despite being a
major technological breakthrough at the time, the
large blast furnaces of the 18th century continued to
require huge amounts of charcoal. It was only in the
19th century that charcoal was no longer needed –
as coke was now used to fire the furnaces.*

2. From the cairn, the path heads E at first to drop down from
Blawith Knott. It then swings left and drops into a dip. Beyond
here, it climbs slightly and then passes to the right of a tiny tarn.
The path winds its way in and out of clusters of heather-covered
rock and patches of bracken. When it swings sharp left, turn right

along a narrower trail heading gently uphill (E).

3. Climb easily to the next cairn on top of a small hill above Tottlebank. Dropping down the other side, you pick up a grassy path heading NNE. Turn left along a clear path cutting straight across your downward route. At the next path junction, turn right to continue downhill (NE). The track briefly swings NW before resuming its downward trend.

4. Before long, you drop to a solid bridleway close to the bottom of a lonely valley. Turn left here and, in about 0.6km, bear left at a clear fork. The gravel-covered bridleway goes off to the right, heading downhill, but your route heads slightly uphill – on a wide, grassy swathe through the bracken.

5. Having forded a particularly wide beck, you join another path coming up from the right. Just after passing a farmhouse at Spunham, the wall on your right swings away down the hill. The main path keeps close to the wall, but you should now take the narrow trail off to the left through the bracken (SW).

6. Turn left at the road. It's now just over 1km along the road back to the Giant's Grave, where the walk started - a steady climb through lovely surroundings.

> *There are lots of signs that Bronze Age people were active in this area. Ancient settlements are dotted about on the fells as are several burial cairns. The Giant's Grave itself is thought to be a Bronze Age barrow. It consists of a shallow hollow in the ground with a single standing stone. Bronze Age people left us some of the most enigmatic of prehistoric remains that can be seen in Cumbria today – stone circles such as mysterious Castlerigg near Keswick and Sunkenkirk near Millom, for example. But what were these stone monuments for? Were they religious sites, trading posts, calendars? We may never know...*

8

Claife Heights
and Windermere lakeshore

This meandering walk to the west of Windermere visits a couple of beautifully located tarns before entering the forests of Claife Heights. This route is a joy at all times of the year, although it is particularly spectacular on a clear autumn day when the trees are changing colour and the views across to the Langdales from Wise Een Tarn are simply breathtaking. But this area also has a darker side – walk the tracks at dusk and you might hear an eerie call coming from the heart of the forest or, worse still, you may even be unlucky enough to come across the mysterious hooded figure of the Claife Crier. You have been warned!

Start/Finish: National Trust pay and display car park on the B5285 (SD387953). This is about 5.5km south-east of Hawkshead. If you're coming across Windermere from Bowness on the ferry, it's just less than 0.6km from the Ferry House, to the right of the road.
Distance: 9.7km (6 miles)
Height gain: 284m (930ft)

1. Take the path heading SW from the car park, alongside a wall on your left and heading towards Hill Top and the Sawreys. Once through the next gate, cross the road and pick up the continuation of the path on the other side. After the next gate, walk along the B5285 into Far Sawrey. When the road bends left, turn right along a rough track.

2. Cross straight over a surfaced track and go through a kissing-gate. You soon join another surfaced lane close to a riding school. Keep straight ahead. When the lane bends left, pick up a narrow path and walk with the wall on your right. Go through a metal kissing-gate and then drop down the shady track.

3. Turn right along the road, passing the Sawrey Hotel, and take the next road turning on your right (Cuckoo Brow Lane). About 130 metres after crossing a cattle grid, bear left along a track that slowly climbs to Moss Eccles Tarn.

> *Beatrix Potter bought Moss Eccles Tarn in 1913, the year she married local solicitor William Heelis. The couple kept a boat on the tarn and spent many happy summer evenings here – he fishing, she sketching. They also planted one red water lily and one white water lily. It is now a Site of Special Scientific Interest with a range of aquatic plants as well as damselflies and dragonflies.*

4. Beyond this pretty spot, the track continues climbing until you reach a gate. You now have a superb view of the Langdales and the mountains to the south and west of Mickleden. Wise Een Tarn, just in front of you, forms a lovely foreground should you fancy taking a few snaps. After passing a smaller, dammed tarn on your right, the path climbs a grassy slope and then enters the forest via a gate.

> *It now seems appropriate to warn you about the Claife Crier – before you head any deeper into the dark forest... One stormy night, a long, long time ago, the ferrymen of Windermere heard an eerie voice summoning them from the western shores of the lake. Most chose to ignore the call, but one young oarsman set off to collect his fare. He returned several hours later, ashen-faced and struck dumb. What had happened to him out there on the lake? What had he seen? His colleagues never found out for he soon developed a fever and, within days, was dead. The voice continued to call out from the Claife Heights on wild nights, but the ferrymen ignored it. Finally, a priest was called in to exorcise it – and the spirit was silenced, supposedly banished to a quarry.*
>
> *There have been several theories to explain the origins of the so-called Claife Crier. It has been suggested that it was*

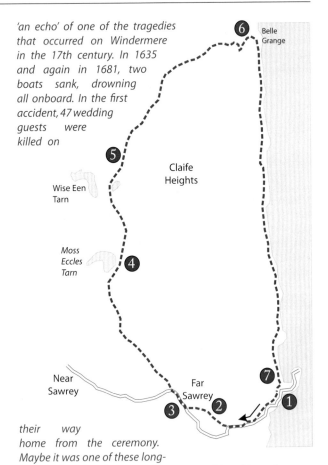

'an echo' of one of the tragedies that occurred on Windermere in the 17th century. In 1635 and again in 1681, two boats sank, drowning all onboard. In the first accident, 47 wedding guests were killed on

Belle Grange

Claife Heights

Wise Een Tarn

Moss Eccles Tarn

Near Sawrey

Far Sawrey

their way home from the ceremony. Maybe it was one of these long-lost revellers that the young ferrymen saw? Local legend has it that the calls came from the ghost of a monk from Furness Abbey who was prevented from marrying the woman he loved by his monastic vows. Tormented, he retreated to the forests of Claife where he died of grief.

> *Some people claim to have seen his hooded figure wandering the forest tracks after dark.*

5. Follow the clear track into the forest for about 350 metres and then turn left along a narrow, stony trail. When this crosses a clear forest track, keep heading straight downhill. Eventually, you reach a surfaced forest road. Cross straight over and head down the rough track opposite, towards Belle Grange. At a T-junction near to the lakeshore, turn right along the clear track, towards Ferry House.

6. After about 3.5km of lakeshore walking, turn right at a road junction. Almost immediately, go through a gap in the wall on your right. This climbs through the trees, providing lovely views down Windermere. Just before you reach the unstable ruins of Claife Station, turn left down some stone steps.

> *Claife Station was built in the 1790s as a place for tourists to enjoy the views of Windermere. It was particularly fashionable in the 1830s and '40s when parties and dinners were held here. The drawing room windows were its most famous feature, each with a different view and with tinted glass that was designed to recreate natural lighting effects. Yellow represented summer, orange was for autumn, light green for spring and light blue for winter. There was also a dark blue for moonlight and a lilac tint to give the impression of a storm.*

7. At the bottom, turn right, still following signs for Hill Top, and you soon re-enter the car park where the walk started.

9

Carron Crag

Carron Crag (314m) is by far the highest point in the sprawling Grizedale Forest. There is hardly anything else above 300m within a two-mile radius, so it feels like you're on top of Cumbria when you reach this point. Climbing gradually, the route follows forest tracks for most of the way, but there is also a long section of road walking at the end.

Start/Finish: Machell's Coppice car park, 0.8km south of Brantwood on the eastern shore of Coniston Water (SD309951)
Distance: 9.5km (5.9 miles)
Height gain: 323m (1,060ft)

---

1. Turn left out of the car park and walk along the road. After about two-thirds of a kilometre, cross the stile beside the gate on your left a little way back from the road. If you reach a building, you've gone too far along the road.

2. The track climbs steadily through the forest. After fording a beck, it follows a gully that becomes a stream in wet conditions. As you emerge from this gully, you will pass a small stone building on your left. You briefly follow the route of one of the Forestry Commission's waymarked walks – indicated by purple-topped posts. Just before the purple route drops to ford a beck, turn right up an old forestry track that is now grassed-over.

> *The Forestry Commission's immense Grizedale Forest Park stretches for miles – from Hawkshead in the north to Satterthwaite and beyond in the south, an area of 2,447 hectares. In recent years, it has become extremely popular with mountain-bikers, who flock to the area to*

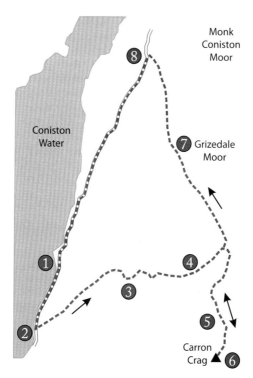

take advantage of a wide range of routes available – from the wide, gravel forest roads to the purpose-built North Face trail. This challenging, 16-kilometre route, intended for more adventurous mountain-bikers, includes plenty of winding single-track, bermed turns and boardwalk sections.

3. Turn left along the wide forest road at the top. You will soon pass a fingerpost indicating this is the way to High Bank Ground. Keep to this track until, just after the buildings at Lawson Park, you turn right along a stony track heading up through the forest. About 250m beyond

41

Lawson Park, bear left at a fork – along the wider of the two trails.

4. Turn left along a wide forest road. Finally, the slog up through the trees pays off as the views open out – towards the Kentmere fells to the NE and the Howgills over to the E. Take the next wide track on your right, but remember this junction, because you will return to it after the climb on to Carron Crag. Ignore the next path on your left; simply continue climbing steadily.

5. Soon after passing and ignoring a wide forest road off to the right, the track bends left. As it does so, cross the stile on your right. This narrower path now climbs to the summit of Carron Crag, a lump of uninspiring, grey rock with a trig pillar crowning it. It's a short, easy scramble to the trig pillar, but take care because the rocks can get very slippery in wet weather.

6. From the summit, retrace your steps down to the stile, beyond which you turn left. When you reach the T-junction where you first joined this wide track, turn right and then, almost immediately, fork left – towards High Cross. You will soon see the North Face mountain bike trail off to your right and, a little way after that, the track forks. Bear left here, along the slightly narrower route. You now need to watch for a tiny section of wall just to the right of the track. A few metres after this, bear left at an indistinct fork, heading down a winding, stony track.

7. About 700m after this fork, you cross a bridge. Be careful that you don't go through the gate on your left here; you need to follow the track round to the right. After the next major beck, the track swings sharp left, through a gate and reaches the road near Lanehead Outdoor Education Centre.

8. Turn left along the road and follow it for 2.2km back to the car park, passing Brantwood along the way and with Coniston Water on your right. It's a quiet road, but it is narrow and winding, so you need to be careful.

Brantwood was the home of the great Victorian intellectual John Ruskin. He was born in London in 1819, and first visited the Lake District when he was five years old. He once said that the "first thing I remember as an event in life was being taken by my nurse to the brow of Friar's Crag on Derwentwater". It was, he continued, "the creation of the world for me". He made his home on the shores of Coniston Water in 1872 and lived there until he died in 1900.

One of the most influential thinkers of his age, he wrote more than 250 works on subjects as diverse as literary criticism, social theory, the history of art, mythology, ornithology and pollution. Containing a strong desire to improve conditions for the poor, his ideas had a profound effect on the early development of the Labour Party in Britain. His many fans included Marcel Proust and Mahatma Gandhi, who translated Ruskin's Unto This Last, a damning critique of capitalist economics, into Gujarati. Leo Tolstoy described him as "one of the most remarkable men, not only of England and of our own time, but of all countries and all times".

Ruskin did a lot of work to 18th-century Brantwood, including the construction of the south-west turret, which gave him a magnificent view of the lake. He filled his home with works of art and items that he had brought back from his travels. There were pre-Raphaelite paintings, watercolours by Turner, medieval manuscripts and a large collection of minerals, many of which visitors can still see today.

10

HOLME FELL

At a mere 317m, Holme Fell provides some surprisingly grand views of the Lake District, particularly the Langdale Pikes. Although this is probably the toughest walk in the book because of the number of steep slopes involved, the walking is not too hard – suitable, perhaps, for older children. There is, however, plenty of potential to get lost on Holme Fell, so you need to keep your wits about you as you negotiate the maze of paths on this small lump of heathery crags and bracken-covered slopes.

Start/Finish: National Trust pay and display car park at Tom Gill
on the A593, about 3km north of Coniston (SD321999)
Distance: 7.7km (4.8 miles)
Height gain: 299m (980ft)

---

1. Turn left out of the car park and walk along the main road for about 200 metres. Take the next turning on your right – towards Yew Tree Farm – but just before you enter the farmyard itself, turn right through the gate.

Yew Tree Farm, built in 1693, was used as a setting in Miss Potter, the 2006 Beatrix Potter biopic starring Renée Zellwegger. The farm was one of many owned in the Lake District by Potter, but in the film it becomes Hill Top, now her most famous property. The National Trust had invited the director to use the real Hill Top, but on visiting the Near Sawrey property, the designer, Martin Childs, realised that it would be too restrictive. He then had to convince the National Trust that Yew Tree Farm was a preferable location. On the concept drawing that he showed to the charity, he drew what he described as a "monster pig" with lots of piglets wandering around freely. His plan was to scare the National Trust into believing that the pigs, an essential part of any 'Hill Top' scenes, would destroy the real Hill Top's beautiful heritage garden.

2. The track swings left and, as the wall on your right ends, turn right along a rough track. You quickly go through a kissing-gate and then, when the quad bike track swings right, keep straight ahead on a narrow path between some low knolls. As the gap between the knolls narrows, don't be tempted down to the right; maintain height and you soon go through a gate in the fence, beyond which the path swings right.

3. When you reach a large boulder to the right of the path, bear left to head uphill through sparse woodland. The climb is short, but moderately steep, sometimes on loose stone. After about 350 metres of climbing, don't be tempted by a narrow trail off to the right through the bracken; keep to the most obvious path as it swings left to climb through a shallow gully.

4. At the top of the rise, you step over what looks like the remains of an old wall and are suddenly welcomed by the glorious sight of the Langdale Pikes to the NW. Turn left at the large cairn to climb to the first of the Holme Fell summit cairns. There are paths all over the place here, but you shouldn't go wrong if you simply keep heading uphill. When the gradient finally eases, swing left to climb to the first cairn. The views from here are impressive, particularly to the E and NE: the Fairfield fells, Ill Bell and even the Howgills are clearly visible.

5. Look over to the left now and you will see Holme Fell's true summit. To reach it, you must turn your back on the cairn, and, with Coniston Water stretching on ahead of you, walk S for about 15m and then turn right along a faint path through a gap between two knolls (NW veering W). This drops to a dip where the path forks. Bear left (SW) and then, almost immediately, bear right to climb steeply. The last

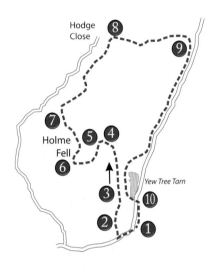

Hodge Close

Holme Fell

Yew Tree Tarn

part of the ascent is a bit of a clamber on bare rock, but you quickly reach the cairn and its uninterrupted views of Wetherlam and the Coniston fells.

6. From the cairn, take the path heading N. When it soon splits, bear left (NNW, veering N) to begin descending steeply on grass. At the next fork, bear right to continue steeply downhill. When you reach a slightly clearer path, bear left along it – in the general direction of the Langdales in the distance (NNE, veering N).

7. Eventually, you drop down through a lightly wooded area and on to a track near a wall. Turn right along this track, ignoring another track heading up to the right in a short while. You will go through a gate/stile and, soon after, there is a stile to the left. The main route actually continues along the track, but if you cross the stile here, you will be able to see the huge, sheer-sided pits left behind by the Hodge Close slate workings. Be careful here, particularly if you have dogs or young children, because the pits are unfenced.

> Coniston's slate has been worked since Roman times, although historians know little about the industry before the end of the 17th century. Despite fierce competition from Welsh slate, great expansion took place in the early part of the 19th century, and the industry received a massive boost when, in 1859, the railway reached Coniston. Sadly though, this was short-lived – and the

industry's decline began in the 1880s.

World War One, in particular, caused huge problems for quarries such as Hodge Close. With the skilled men away at war, the steep walls became unstable and rock falls started to occur, damaging equipment. Eventually, the pumps were stopped and water began to fill the pits. Quarrying restarted when the men returned, but then World War Two began and the pits deteriorated again. Hodge Close was finally closed in the 1950s.

8. Continuing along the track with the quarry fence on your left, you will eventually reach a rough lane. Turn right here, towards High Oxenfell. Beyond the farmhouse, the track goes over to asphalt. When it forks, bear right.

9. Just before you reach the A593, go through the kissing-gate on your right, towards Glen Mary Bridge. The path now runs parallel with the road, along the base of Holme Fell. About 1.3km after joining the path – and having passed a couple of gates providing access to the road on your left – you reach a signpost in the woods, close to Yew Tree Tarn. Keep straight ahead (SW) through the trees. The signpost indicates that you are following the circuit of the tarn, but there isn't a path on the ground at this point. When you reach the wall, however, you pick up a good path that skirts the western edge of the tarn and then crosses the dam at its southern end.

Yew Tree Tarn was another of the Marshall family's creations. It was dammed by James Marshall's grandson Aubrey in 1923.

10. Turn right along the main road and, in a few metres, pick up a path to the left, through the trees. This runs parallel with the road and later crosses the bridge over Tom Gill to return to the car park.

Other titles by
QUESTA PUBLISHING LIMITED

LAKE DISTRICT
WALKS WITH CHILDREN
Buttermere and the Vale of Lorton
Around Coniston
Keswick and the Newlands Valley
Ambleside
Grasmere
Ullswater
Around Kendal
Around Windermere
South Lakeland

EASY RAMBLES
Around Keswick and Borrowdale
Around Ambleside and Grasmere
Around Eskdale
Around Wasdale
Around Dunnerdale
Around Coniston and Hawkshead
Around Patterdale and Ullswater
Around Langdale
Around Ennerdale and Calder Valley

YORKSHIRE DALES
WALKS WITH CHILDREN
Wharfedale
Swaledale
Wensleydale
Malham and Airedale
Ribblesdale

PEAK DISTRICT
WALKS WITH CHILDREN
Dark Peak

PENNINES
SHORT WALKS
Eden Valley and North Pennines

All QUESTA titles are available from
27 Camwood, BAMBER BRIDGE, Lancashire PR5 8LA
or by FAX to
0705 349 1743

www.questapublishing.co.uk